Lyle Neff

IVANHOE STATION

Ivanhoe Station

poems by

lyle neff

ANVIL PRESS PUBLISHERS

Printed and bound in Canada
First Edition
Cover design: JT Osborne
Cover photo: Dennis E. Bolen
Author photo: Amber Ridington

Canadian Cataloguing in Publication Data

Neff, Lyle.
Ivanhoe station
Poems.
ISBN 1-895636-16-7
I. Title
PS8577.E335I92 1997   C811'.54   C97-910202-2
PR9199.3.N335I92 1997

Some of these poems were previously published in
*Prism International, sub-TERRAIN, Adbusters Quarterly,
Canadian Dimension, Seventh Wave* and *Tremor.*

Represented in Canada by the Literary Press Group
Distributed by General Distribution Services

Anvil Press
Suite 204A—175 East Broadway,
Vancouver, BC
Canada   V5T 1W2

CONTENTS

POEMS

for

The MacKenzie-Papineau Battalion

Bribing The Cherubim

FABLE FOR CENTRAL AMERICA

I

700 times
their little guns
burst

peasant thongs
snickered on
Presidential floors

but El Presidente was gone

II

the guerrillas enlisted
his fat daughter

to serve rum
& coffee in
crystal glasses &
her underwear

but El Presidente was missing

the new army
hanged his wife
& awarded to

her hungry children
his ten thousand medals

but El Presidente had left

III

the broken-legged priest
remembered a hymn:
if rich man you cannot
enter heaven try to see
with the needle's eye
use its blade to butcher
your camel & bribe
the cherubim with camel filet
then if you dare rich man

foxtrot with the astounded angels

IV

El Presidente's dancing shoes
have now been nationalized

THE AMNESIA BRIGADES

I

Isn't all change cataclysmic? The money
you spend for lottery tickets at the Chinese grocery,
the glimpse of an airliner at dusk, the path
through dense woods like a greasy thumbprint in cake;
doesn't each memory destroy all others, illumination
of death inside you?

II

He's forgotten, lodge brothers intoned of my grandpa,
more than you'll ever know. Ten years old, respectful,
I'd hear the paterfamilias speak: *Black-faced bastards,*
he'd say, *are taking over. But war, especially race war,
is nature's way of keeping population down.* Many years
it took me to understand how he'd frightened me, made me
what I am. My friend tells me *her* grandfather
was a lifelong Communist. Remember Communists?
This paterfamilias would never have the word *Stalin*
mentioned in his presence. He died that way,
my friend says, Stalin an empty space in his head.
The same blank place is in me, of course,
an opposite to racial memory: ancestry we wish to forget.

III

Patriotism, the Japanese often say, is the memory
of foods eaten in childhood. I must contrast my theory
that amnesia's the fuel of Americans, evangelists
and terrorists. Remember this: a great desire
nourishes the act of forgetting. I lose my keys
three times a day—because I'm *tired* of goddamned keys;
they only remind me of the rudders
on the ships I've dreamed.

IV

The difference between an alcoholic in a blackout
and a normal, drug-free human of conscience
—say, Adolf Eichmann or Marc Lepine—is that
the alcoholic cannot remember what's to be denied
and is generally too shaky to commit suicide.
So we blackout artists always get caught, and only later
do we learn for what. No doubt it'll be a Sunday
when the temperance police haul me from my sodden bed
and kneecap me for the thousand crimes I've forgotten;
or a gunman will kick in the classroom door
and shoot out the lights, shouting it was you,
I knew it was you, glass crashing everywhere,
the newly-dead falling to earth—and I'll cry *what?*
and the sun will burst right through me.

DEATH SQUAD POEM

This moment has ended, strange woman;
I mean your dissident Millennium.
Your pamphlets say JUSTICE, your eyes
Indifference.
I am nothing so simple as a predator.

I am Securitate.
I am Central Intelligence.
I am Cheka,

The smiling one with clean fingernails.
I am your solicitous escort from Room 101
To that muddy ditch where no nation rules.

For the State creates itself, my late
Advocate, as in this curious profession
I create myself, as you once created yourself
In your tawdry rebellions—to no avail.

When I displayed my identification, your lips
Parted like clouds, and that was when I knew;
I embraced your so-small throat,
I set the metal to your wondrous eye—

Ah, there was never doubt.
My State ordains nothing
But beauty. Lovely woman,
Remember what I am—
Simply function

RIEL'S LAST LETTER FROM VANCOUVER

Mon cher Gabriel,

It is raining here. I imagine
that pleases you. Forgive me,
but I will not be returning;
all that is east of here still
seems shaped like a gallows.

There are no mounted armies in Kitsilano,
no rifles, no trenches, no pemmican.
Merely damp streets unrolled
like the tongues of chameleons,
arranged to weavework for our pleasure.

Sometimes, Gabriel, the drunkards
race their cars, or stop and scream
at midnight near my home on West Third.
Do you think I sleep easily? I awake
incoherent, with visions of the rope,
of the noose, of the war and the CPR.

But in this city I am well beloved,
having promised no incitement to change,
no television endorsements; certainly no rage.
I have promised. But yesterday, Gabriel,

they nailed up Lévèsque
in front of that cafe on Broadway.

Crumpled old René! A white man,
but possessed of Métis spine.
They draped his little form in dogwood
and the old polemics clenched at my throat;
I wanted to make a speech, Gabriel!
Because you know me; whenever I die,
I get new ideas. But when I stared in his yellow eyes,
I forgot my French, every word. Forgive me,
but I shall not be returning.
Gabriel, I am popular here. I am
a curiosity, so long as I remain quiet.

Here's an irony for you, *mon cher*. I go often,
in the evenings, to a stretch of warm sand
named English Bay,
I bring cocaine, and sometimes a woman friend
who laughs in English at words like these
and kisses my unlikely hand.

Je me souviens,
Louis David Riel.

WAITING FOR A CHEQUE

Poverty's weight makes a sea creature of you;
Gilled, scaly and scant with the pressure
You drift along the bottom where the current is slow,
Where Gastown curls into the Downtown Eastside.
The old black woman in her charismatic hat
Sings a hymn at you, while you hunt up a used transfer,
While office workers steam and churn, while light
Pours itself uselessly, without reflection,
Onto the old Woodward's charred-black windows.
Each cloud resembles a decent pouch of tobacco,
A plate of bacon and eggs, an endlessly refilled
Cup of coffee—*coffee!* You'd burn a saint for coffee
In the middle of the month, 11 cold and fluid days to go.

BRAND LOYALTY POEM

So this splendid huckster cries *baby c'mere I love you*
She's become the best gesture in the land & her hand's
In my heart—I'm ready to believe, always believe
Naturally because she's shot in soft focus
She lilts without static & she wants me
To buy just a few things—

Like razor blades, Luvs diapers, soap & dry gin
Manly cigarettes, fast cars & feminine hygiene
Deodorant, shampoo, some Alpo for the cat
& new sweaters, jeans, snappy dark Coke
Lipstick, a government & some lo-cal yogurt
Rice Krispies & toupees, some morality & hurt
Computers, perfumes, $200 running shoes
Compact discs, financial contempt & leg wax
(Historians will look back & say
That's how the world sang in those days)
Tours to the Sudan & Gatorade for thirst
Vacuum cleaners, toilet plungers & Sun-Kist
(I believe, believe this sweet propagandist
I need, I need to be taught how to feel)
Bedsheets & vitamins, sturdy chairs by Ikea
Bathing suits & infant formula & Revlon eyes
Molson's love if you want it, IBM's warmth if you're lonely

So maybe she's diluted her passion
Thinned it across ten million screens

19

But I like this artificial woman, I want
To go where she takes me, I'll just tuck my wallet
In past my ribs where my heart used to be,
& let money & time & language
Tick away in false blood until I disappear

The Lioness
of Vancouver

ON THE CHANCE OF A PROMOTION

Listen, each morning she's near to me,
Nose a bit bent, eyes muddy and tragic,
Cheap black runners on her minuscule feet,
Long and many-ringed fingers drumming
With the Number 14's engine as it coughs
Near Main

Her fluid and yellow hair, certain
Against her black and inevitable coat,
Makes me get up and clean myself and go
Each A.M. to nobly disregard her perfection,
Her bit of light squeaking through December,
She herself The Lioness of Vancouver

And me another lonely swine, my hand
On the silver bar, pretending not to look—
Not that she's ever seen me—
The next red-eyed suitor of the Number 14,
One who works, who tries without ambition,
A man who doesn't sell.

TO BE KISSED

I can't remember a time when it was trivial.
The first time, it caught all my attention,
Like Northern Lights, those stately whispers,
Like a wedding procession led by horses,
Like the promise of fulfillment in a thousand books
I had yet to read. It was something I knew
I would live with. Well,

It was tawdry as well, elemental, made me hoarse
To think of all the women who could be kissing me
But weren't. When I was kissed I broke, I flashed
Like a circuit breaker, awoke distant cities
With the sound of a bell ringing and, in sum,
Astonished the masses with my heartfelt endorsement
Of the kiss. Then,

When kisses were for a time in short supply,
I expounded my holistic theory of the kiss:
I praised kissing with tongues, with dental plates,
The symbolism of the occasional bite, I explained
How kisses ought never to be in short supply, and why
Gift horses should not be kissed. I even wrote a poem
Or two about it, lips bruised with simple delight.

ODE TO JESSICA'S HAT

Listen, some hats
Stay at rest; but not
Jessica's hat. Jessica's hat
Acts.

O brain-warmer, black felt smile with her head
In your belly, O shield against the moon's unkind songs,
Keeper of riddles and lint, O head piece among headgear;
What's a hat for? To know eternity? Even gods,
Having spent twenty minutes drying their divine hair,
Are loath to get it wet. Jessica's hat tightens at the brim,
Sneers at the drizzle, wraps its arms around her scalp—

While I walk with them, my head wet as a swamp,
And tell the tale of turbans and helmets, cloth caps
And kaffiyeh, the tiara and bowler and yarmulka too;
I sing for Jessica all kindnesses of the protected head,
The inevitable worth of it, of haberdashery,
The ineluctable modality of hatness.

ONE CONDITIONAL UTOPIA

Once, wholly inside you while the sun burned,
Once, drunk in the afternoon with friends
Watching some noisy movie a room away, once
Sex became the engine, the sole and limited heaven.

Then the white line of your shoulders was the horizon
& I rose full above it, a sweaty & crumpled moon.
We strained & buckled, wings of linen beating, for
We were faster than the tides & of more consequence.

Outside a child cried *I win, I win*: & near us were
Our summer clothes & the hole I'd kicked in the closet,
A web flapping from it now, forsaken by spiders:
On it groaned, our limited heaven, the libidinal engine.

NOTES ON YEARNING FROM THE
PUBLIC RELATIONS MAN

God damn all these Templars and Crusaders
These contemptible imperialists and cavaliers
God damn them and their endless posing
The Holy Grail doesn't *want* to be found

What Madame Grail wants is a margarita
A Bloody Mary or Purple Jesus or even better
A waist to wrap her thighs around
On the first day of summer

And if you'd spent the centuries
As a target, been sought after forever
Like a piece of the Virgin's ass
You'd need a vacation too

The Holy Grail may have been a courtesan
But she never was a prima donna
And she is tired of morons with swords
Who kill perfectly functional dragons

Madame Grail does not wish her name called
By Christian rapists or Muslim torturers
Or Jewish terrorists or anyone in love
She is finished with victims and predators

Picture the Holy Grail in sunglasses and sarong
Dodging paparazzi in the airport of the heart.

CONQUERING

Alexander the Great fell hard in love
(The numb bastard had thought
There were no more worlds to conquer)
He died in a darkened movie house
Eating the oil-soaked popcorn of those days
Eyes red-lined and his mind full of thighs
No more worlds to conquer
What bullshit
He didn't even deserve her

LOVE FOR BEGINNERS

first you stand up and get picked to pieces so
you fall down and repair yourself
stitched together you crawl in a new direction
and something impossible falls on your head
for a time you are ugly and it is your fault

then you give off the light everybody wants
every room is there because you are in it
you are scattered over a city
and you hear your name in many languages
by now you are becoming impossibly thin

soon you are tacked to a wall and commented upon
you are becoming historical—somehow present
but solely the preoccupation of scholars
with all your strength you strive to escape and see
and your eyes boil with the hottest fire of sight

you burn everything your vision falls on
you are happy in your sulphurous way
you are free for a time and then doused
you trickle screaming away through the ashes
and then you stand up

ADULTERY POEM

Memory seems the bitch of the process.
Of my screwing around

w/ the parameters.
Memory's a plague, memory etches names
where names don't belong. Isn't the heart

a plastic satellite & saner w/out names?
Names like this: bed. BED:

there's a charge to it. Like a song in Braille
at twilight when yr fingers break & nothing

moves forward & nothing—but fuck that.
Break it. I'm not here

to justify. Bed's a surface
& you someday will fall thru.
Like me you'll fall thru & find

piranhas & great death-shaped
American nuclear submarines. & maybe

yr own faceless self drifting
just like you always wanted

CONTINUAL DREAMS OF FALLING

Yet maybe she's peripheral to the central swings,
The recent terrifying pendulums of life, maybe she
Is not the instigator of the violent shoves
My jangled senses have taken lately, like kids in a riot;

I'm taking coffee so bitter and pure it kicks me
Like a pony, into the next heightenings: sudden blue
Awareness of the veins in everyone's hands, static
Lightning attacks from doorhandles, always sneezing,

And always getting blessed for it. Yet maybe she
Is the fulcrum of this taunting and robustness,
Not just a part of it; when I see her at ease
With her day, I know we are made of steel

That even something long and truly dead can come back
To get a whiff of baby oil, a kiss, a fury of sensation.

A Pale Sentry

PERFECT ACCIDENTS

Poet must be the wrong name for a naked man
Who sits on the toilet reading the Romantics

For when I think *poem* I think garbage
Barges aching across a quiescent sea

And how sunlight moves to make worthwhile
Even this, a boat of bagged catshit,
Feathers and dead hats, used-up pornography

Poem is not the world but our strange
Motions in it, swimming through sewage, dancing
At a wedding with the smallest nieces

PATERFAMILIAS

For a moment my father's hair lifts to the dizzy sky;
The rest of him dozes. He cannot but welcome
This tranquil moment, here on his gentleman's farm;
Cannot but approve of the dry Tanqueray & lemonade
Waiting by his hand.

My father's hand! Railroader's hand, stubby & patched
With scars—who gives it work & shape? My mother
Wanders in the fireweed at the end of the lawn,
Throwing grain to the Peking ducks & singing.
& this half-drunk giant,

My progenitor, might be fireweed himself. It's in the way
He is rooted & yet swaying, somehow in the blue eyes,
Tangled brows & slow-thickening body I inherited—
But fireweed, fireweed at sunset, is a long blossom
& John Jason Neff is a short man.

Who gives form & history to this diminutive atheist,
My father, who loads his paunch onto weight machines,
To bicycle & exercise for his heart's sake—but then
Sits on his patio guzzling gin? My mother is lovely
In her easy labours & printed dress,

Lovelier still in the quixotic methods of her hand
As she tends criminal children & a wayward garden.
My mother's hand! But I must ask her. Shall we keep him

Here like this, asleep in a lawn chair before his house,
Toyed with by a minor breeze?

Mother, he is a handsome old man when he drinks at sunset;
But he's stubborn like me & does not believe his name
To be rhythmic. Mother, take my hand; straighten
The grey hairs of this man, old badger, husband & sire;
We should lift him from this sphere

Into whatever gin-laced universe
Antiquated railroaders might believe in.

IN THE PLACE YOU WERE BORN
YOUR SOUND CONTINUES

Places I've been, hotels, lakes,
Mountains and corner stores—they stay with me,
Like a much beloved leather coat
Grown one million miles long.
It's a wonder I don't trip,

Garbed in such distances, eternal sidewalks,
Stratospheric heights of stairs,
A burning house or two, a number of beds
(And beds have burned too); still
I walk forward, still I think of the past

As it struggles to catch up,
As it waves like a young drunken uncle
Back from the city with new rock and roll records
And a red-haired young woman whose smallest breath
Makes you grow one million miles wide. Yes,

The past is my entourage, I'm a celebrity of Time!
And the places I've been, green glacial hills,
Phone booths and abandoned mines, they still spin
In orbit round my aging centre, drawing me out,
Making real all my breadth and height,

Until the time of unwinding, the moment I die,
In some quiet city of the next century,
In the grandeur of time and place,
One million days of light.

JOHNNY AT THE MOVIES

Nothing deters him. Not the scent of butter,
Not the stoned flashlight-men in soldier suits,
Not even the sleepy old velvet that means
To make him dream. He will not dream,
Not at management's behest. For he's irretrievable,

Shaken up with music, words, nerves. Somewhere
Under his long hair, behind his always wounded face,
He knows every name in the credits. Johnny is moved
By all that moves; the eye that loves cannot discriminate.

So he stands, a pale sentry in the projectionist's beam,
And from his gestures two shadow-hands on screen begin
To undress a woman who is made of light: one dream
Flaring into another.

THE WHEELS

The rickshaw driver is dead. It was last week
when his tattered muscles abandoned his bones.
He sang his brave aria on the theme of weakness
& drifted to the cobbles like a lonely crow.
The rickshaw man is dead

& I must do his living for him. It is painful
to roll back the great stone of his ending; painful
to make a lie of his epitaph. To become him is
at once mad & essential. When a rickshaw man dies

This world flinches. Or should. My wife says such work
is vanity, emptiness; I put down my pen & tell her,
It is not. Does a dead man need a poem? Is there honour
or use for him in painting & singing?

I will not bend again to such ritual. Only deeds now
in testimony to my good *doppelgänger*; only movement,
only action will suffice for the death of the rickshaw man.
Tonight I go into the city.

I may have famous passengers: Christina the actress,
avatar of scandal & jewellery; our Lord Mayor,
who in his heart must balance our city; perhaps my wife
& that questionable man, her new lover.

For this reunion leaves my harness ruined with sweat,
sandals & feet in perfect blood communion. The rickshaw
is a twisted mouth & I its hunger:
& the rickshaw man is alive.

BUSTED TUESDAY

Today everyone got a divorce.
The men all walked like cripples,
All the women were walking away.
This was in the rainy West End,
Where mirrored towers must look
At each other all day long. Now,
I am remote from this—it is November
And even if the day is broken I must work—

But I saw today a clever shop window
In which The Invisible Man was besieged
By a squadron of colourful ties. I laughed,
And beside me a husband and wife hated.
You know who it is they hated—
They crackled like a pair of radios,
Their November divorce begun. Busted Tuesday

Was like a wind pulling down the electric lines,
All our power lying treacherous in the streets.

WRITING HAPPINESS

Dear explicit emotion:

It is the season now when you return,
Shouldering through the ruins
And singing for no reason, everywhere
One feels this splendid rumour

Even the burn-scarred woman on the bus
Tells passengers of your return, how her stride
Has unaccountably lengthened, and suddenly
She is intrigued by everyone's hair

At work the machines burble like infants,
Accounts rendered in logarithms and blank verse,
Security consultants have been seen touching
Each other, and artificial plants are thriving

For you have been seen in the mountains, the suburbs,
South of the border and near the city limits,
Riding in trucks, on elephants, on ferries
You have been seen, if never described exactly

Your absence has been just what you'd expect,
Malnourished, erratic, pugnacious and lonely,
But we have put up signs announcing your imminence,
Everything is unlocked, it is the season of your return

Please hurry before it all falls apart,
Yours searchingly,

All of us

THE LAUGHTER OF MANY WOMEN
HEARD FROM AN ELEVATOR SHAFT

Yes it is like silver but it is not silver
Yes it is like a river but it does not flow
It is what makes me a vandal

On the third floor after work
After a day spent pushing paper until
It pushes back, after a day worse than wages—

To be a voyeur, now, on this polished floor
With oyster-shell barrettes & eyeliner in mind
& a cage of laughter plummeting beyond me—

To be this thief of their boxed-up delight,
To be a strange clerk the janitor sees laughing
All alone, to be this is akin to sustenance

Poems

YEARS LATER, A WINO NAMED HANSEL
WRITES TO HIS SISTER

If behind me there's a path of words
or forgotten clothing, food crumbs
or towns not as pristine as they might be;

If a line's drawn behind each of us
as we shuffle over the planet, earth scarred
and cross-hatched into illegibility;

Does this help with here and now, cold
city on the last day of the year, will memory
find me a lover or keep me sane? Sister,

I haven't been eaten yet, but all sweet houses
have collapsed around me; death, as I remember,
is a witch's mouth.

THINGS GONE BADLY WRONG

for Quentin Tarantino

Leave it to fate, the victim thinks,
To make the grand gestures, to swallow
And transform our trivial ones. He sat
And had dinner with them, spring rolls
And green tea, some take-out milkshakes
And a bottle of Golden Wedding for later,
They shot him twice in the face and left.
Gang aft agley, he thinks, in a puddle
Of soya sauce and blood, situation normal,
All fucked up, *que sera sera,* what doesn't kill me
Often does anyway. If I had one wish right now,
It wouldn't be life, but one second's insight,
A glance at Disaster's hairy heart, the surge
Of the lake of fire into our quiet world.

WEDDINGS

Half-a-dozen such ceremonies since my birth
Depending how you count. Many times,
Dearly beloved, under sun and church roof,
Many times in the law's dead eyes,
In the sweet echo of religion, many times
I've helped them get hitched, spilled the wine,
Joined the chorus to give a simultaneous fuck-you
To human clumsiness, to eternity, to everything
We think we know. For I am loyal to all chains,
To the courage fiction requires;
And I believe in marriage.

DRINKING WITH THE BRITISH

Out of an Empire's carcass and on a tsunami of gin
This flotsam washes up. All that discretion erased
By the ocean crossing (an awkward torture
To the soul of an islander), they come impoverished,
Clothed only in alcohol and bile—bile, yes,
For British venom is among the vilest.
There is a flat irony to an English face,

A sarcastic bend to the bony hands that always know
How to draft a cruel letter and roll the cheapest tobacco.
If the stark and huge Canadian sunlight falls right,
A properly blotto Canuck can see Roundheads,
Coal mines, murky histories they wear lightly,
The swine. But what's to envy? These are refugees
Of a sort, exiles from bad food and soccer murders;

From Beijing to Vancouver, they only seek central heating,
Dental care, a tolerable pub. In Canada, it's camping
They want; they're as crazed about the bush as the booze.
It's Mrs Moodie and her hubby redux, and Lowry after that,
Bits and pieces *ad mari usque ad mare* that are forever
England. But who are they now, rambling the raunchy world,
Drinking dry their former colonies and making bad puns?

The British abroad have a love for words,
A badly used idealism with which to endure
The carpings of adolescent nations; their tolerance
Is often mistaken for fatigue; British lies

Have considerably more resonance than British truth, for
The sad old poetry of centuries lies bound up
In their rickety accents. And the British, the British
Almost always die by drowning.

SEEDS

Boondoggles and pitfalls of my adolescence!
I remember how love's merest luminescence
or any rumour of wedding whiskey would ignite me
from pore to pore, astound me from belly to knees—
I know I'd convulse and shout, if ever there was silence;
I remember how I was in my precocious decadence.

Too weak to say *fuck* in my poems of nothing but,
wild for hands in my jeans, deflowerings in trucks,
snap of ozone, licorice-flavour bodies and the cold
that gave frosted beards to we beardless jackals, we old
symptoms of a permanent disease; young, I could name
all that I despised, the faces I wanted to maim—

I knew myself that way. Who could foresee farewell
to the lake or 19th Avenue? What amnesiac spell
tried to erase Juniper, Samantha, Smithers itself?
Didn't I have a bear's heart then, when just a whelp?
Were those days not huge to me? Now I remember
only this: how the bear's heart had bone at its centre.

NOSTALGIA FOR GONDWANALAND

for Marin

The rough but true resemblances of DNA,
The similarities I bear to jackal, jellyfish & jasmine,
Make all of evolution nothing but one eon-spanning
Family reunion. The sort of gig where one says
To a familiar chordate, *Haven't we met before?*
Well, not formally, but genetically. *Ah, I see.*
Oh, it starts badly enough, this clowning cocktail party
Of the persevering biosphere, as mules speak seriously
With august fertility doctors—but the insect cousins
Drink grasshoppers in shiniest attire! Here,
The family squabble between whales & plankton is,
After a few shots of primordial booze, declared over;
& after madrigal singing with my hanging uncles,
The bats, I grow dizzy & exuberant, for we well-armed
Predators have loosened up & suffer amiable mouth-molds
To sprout in our huge teeth! I tell a woozy trilobite,
Listen, it's so good to meet you, 'specially
This near the end—but a matronly bison is having none
Of my apocalyptic maudlinism, though she knows
Sentimentality *is* the mammalian vice. I find myself,
Then, wandering through kelp, seeking the canines
(My secret favourites)—only to find them snoring
In the lap of some huge Jurassic thing, who says,
I've had about enough of you, Jesus H. Sapiens—
& slurredly I tense, for if he's as drunk as me,
Things could get ugly! Elsewhere, there is reptilian

53

Nostalgia for Gondwanaland & an ostrich crows
To a bewigged king penguin: Swimming? Swimming's no job
For avians, cuz. The smart money's on land speed—
Things speed up now, vipers shed tuxedoes in the muck,
Raucous jets of chlorophyll rise high; midnight's
On the family, & come morning we'll find miscegenation
& recrimination & on the floor will be fur & spores,
Scales & feathers & teeth.

BAD FOOD

Today I learned the meaning of "opposite."
I saw a friend of mine inspect his pecs in the mirror—
Worship, I guess, is the word. Then at the Hilltop
Me & my brother had a couple with Uncle Frankie,

Who looked diseased, beaten, obese & tired,
Thank God. My old man's old buddy has no regard
For himself, though much for others; he does not live well
But he lives wholly. Uncle Frankie drinks, fucks & smokes;

Uncle Frankie is revolting in a way, but he does not preen.
He has no slick feathers, nothing to stroke in himself.
Lord knows what he believes in; it is not in his body.
Lord Jesus, I'm always implored to look after myself;

As if I were just a scanty & pimpled biological carriage,
As if physicality & narcissism
Made men from mere flesh!

AN INQUIRY INTO PASSION

Usually it's God, that cripply-ass slavemonger; that,
Or the passionate are yapping through their genitals.
Less often than you'd think, folks get whacked on cash;
Luckily, fiscal passion's so transparently transient
We almost all grow out of it.

But I've seen good women get drunk on the Constitution,
Whole families sundered and bust over whether to cut trees,
Men's lives pissed away for the welfare of another's kid,
And fistfights over dogs. Seems like some things are precious
And if there is a reason we make it.

TIME'S A SLOTH, LOVE'S A MAGGOT

The clock bangs, the cat stomps, the morning
Eats itself, is eaten by an irritated crab,
Then pops back out, grinning. Looks like payday,
Can't be sure. It's like that hiss and yawn of lava
Before the volcano changes everything.
Newspaper's blank but for the weather report,
Which notes that the sky's inside out,
Predicts enmity and bile for late afternoon.
This better be payday. My boots are alive,
Licking each other with soiled tongues. Damn.
I walk on my hands down the mossy streets—
And what time is it? Big and little hands
Do an intricate shake. Looks like
Wishes are horses again, beggars deride
The poor shamefaced nags. Get to the office,
My colleagues are inflatable, my cheque
Cashed itself and went to the city for the weekend.
Unfortunately, when this week ends, there will be
No other. It's complete. There can be nothing else.

LUCKLESS MCKENZIE REPUDIATES THE COSMOS

McKenzie stands at the centre of the universe, pissing
Who, me? Here with my dick out, I'm the apex,
I'm the All? asks he. I don't think so, he answers.
Though once I saw an eclipse, though
I've heard of revolution and spirits—even touched a woman,
I'm still just a guy taking a leak, I have not
The ordering imagination Wallace Stevens spoke of,
I cannot, for chrissakes, even write my name in the snow
Legibly, the great humanists would find me laughable—
& no matter how you shake, wriggle and dance,
That fuckin' last drop always winds up in your pants—
Luckless McKenzie stands at the centre of the universe,
Zipping up.

TRAVELOGUE: THE DEVIL WALKED OVER ME

Hermosillo's heat must have angered him into being.
Sky-touched, garbage-bag-veined and rife with tumbleweed—
I report, I saw him walking hundreds of metres away,
Errant & minuscule cousin of the Mexican storm,
& laughed. The crumbling Pemex, *quesadillas* & Coca-Cola
& all this after three days in the car—

I report, a Canadian in Mexico is apt to neglect the devil.
He pivoted with ease on his single foot, he came for me
& something made me lift my arms; I report, the devil is heat
& a thousand foreign knives; I report, the Mexican devil
Will empty your lungs & strive against you. But
I had to smile, dust in my teeth, stabbed
Again & again in a Mexican gas station,
Thinking of snow.

FALLING WITH HANDS IN POCKETS

Leering at the sexual snow, laughing
At your icy-slick lust, bad driving conditions,
Going down hard on an East Van curb, no chance
To balance, cracking your knee and ankle

Toque yanked over the brows, fierce
Attempt to look fierce, heading to the hovel
Of pleasant solitude and dinner, don't
Fuck with me, and then face-first in the slush

Bag of necessities on your shoulder,
Somebody else's T4, tapes, an apple, necessity
Of taking small steps when the world is ice,
All landing on your head, hands in pockets

The comedians and humanists, passing
In cars and by shank's mare, those who know
That hands were locked in pockets, chipped
Chin and spat of blood and all, jester's pratfall

Choosing while you fall between humiliation
And damage, choosing as much as you like,
Meeting gravity, learning there's never enough time,
Falling with hands in pockets

A DIVERGENCE

Invincible. Bullets break their noses
On my stellar hide, glaciers crack
In fear and turn back, all is as nothing
To my incalculable endurance
And I walk where I will

Shamed. I am foetal and burnt
On this bed, curling round my crimes
In a sick wash, shocked faces
Turning away, guilt and memory
Shall carve me up for their supper

EIDETIC

In fluid and electrics the alligator brain holds it all,
rigid, refined and encyclopedic; the chemical well
contains a green bathing suit, improbable sex acts,
inclusive results from the election of nineteen eighty-six,
a bowl of stinging Thai soup and the origin of scars;
all held static and wet in the ancient clock, the first mind.

So particles mate with forces to render a past,
a coiled rope of ones and zeros renders a self;
are these the details in which God resides?
The newer mind rejects the truth, intolerable and sordid:
that the cries of burned heretics lie encoded
in ashes, that physicality is zero and one, all and nothing.

MONEY AND MUSIC

Ah, it's all math anyway, say the bewigged pontificates
paid to think in symbols, made to ignore the crash
of classes, unable to see how the noise you make
follows from how well you're paid. This leisure society
boogie-woogie, these slavery blues, that military tattoo

It all fits together like a body, so damn near knowable
it makes you cry. My dad's a railroader, I work in restaurants;
he listens—barely—to country twang, while I jump
For rock and roll, I mean I *thrive* on it.
We're union men, Canadians, down on symbolism,
money's dry leash wraps equally round both our necks

But he works it out in weepy angst, while
paranoid aggression is more in his son's line.
Well, our albums are all heaped together now;
we can meet over a bottle of whisky while the rich twitch
to their Mantovani or what-have-you. Maybe
the music's tinny, lacking higher maths, short of soul;
but it's the soundtrack of our lives
and we've paid for it dearly.

LYLE NEFF's work has appeared in *sub-TERRAIN, Prism International, Adbusters Quarterly, Canadian Dimension, Tremor* and *Seventh Wave.* He lives and works in Vancouver.

AUTHOR PHOTO: Amber Ridington